HOW TO BUILD A WINE LIST

Templates, Suggestions, and Tips for Restaurants to Maximize Profits from a Professional Sommelier

MICHELE GARGIULO

Copyright Page
Copyright © 2023 Michele Gargiulo

The rights of Michele Gargiulo to be identified as the author of the work has been asserted by her in accordance with the Copyright Act of America.

All rights reserved.
No part of this book may be reproduced or transmitted in any form or by any means, electronic or mechanical, including photocopying, recording, or by any information storage and retrieval system, without prior permission in writing from the publisher.

For any inquiries or permissions, the publisher can be contacted at sommelierstoriespress@gmail.com.

First published in the United States of America by: Michele Gargiulo

First Print: 2023
Edited by: Teresa Crumpton
Formatted By: Michele Gargiulo
Book Cover Design by: cbooklaunch.com
ISBN: 979-8-9875520-2-5

This book is dedicated to those who are chasing their dreams. Keep learning, I have no doubt you'll get to where you want to be.

This book is meant to advise and give suggestions for building wine lists in restaurants. It is meant to inform those who are working to make a well-balanced wine menu. Following the guides in this book are recommendations to help your business, you must customize the information for your local markets to be successful.

Contents

Chapter 1	1
Why You Want to Optimize Your Wine List	
Chapter 2	4
Who I Am	
Chapter 3	6
Know Your Market	
Chapter 4	9
Selections and Size	
Chapter 5	10
Sommeliers	
Chapter 6	11
Templates with Explanations	
Chapter 7	12
Classically Inspired Wine List Template	
Chapter 8	18
French Inspired Wine List Template	
Chapter 9	23
Italian Inspired Wine List Template	
Chapter 10	29
Asian Inspired Wine List Template	
Chapter 11	35
North American Inspired Wine List Template	
Chapter 12	41
South American Inspired Wine List Template	
Chapter 13	47
Australian Inspired Wine List Template	
Chapter 14	53
Scaling Up Your Menu	
Chapter 15	56
Costs and Pricing	
Chapter 16	59
Can You Use Artificial Intelligence for Your Wine List?	
Chapter 17	61
More Resources to Learn	
Chapter 18	64
Ordering	

Chapter 19   66
Pairings
Chapter 20   68
Extra Wine List Tips

Acknowledgments   71
About the Author   73
Also by Michele Gargiulo   75

Chapter 1
WHY YOU WANT TO OPTIMIZE YOUR WINE LIST

In the restaurants where I've worked, beverage sales accounted for 24 to 30 percent of revenue, depending on the venue. Regardless if it's a small restaurant, or a larger operation, it can translate into big percentages of the overall operation. Beverage sales will have much lower costs than your food costs and typically lead to higher profits. So you'll want to optimize your lists to sell as much wine as possible, pushing more to the profit line.

This book is meant to be a guidebook for you, but keep in mind that all markets are different. The availability of wines are not universal, and you must find what is readily available for you. The laws around purchase and resale can also vary quite a bit so make sure you are following all the laws of your country, state, and county for your wine menu. Obtaining a liquor license also varies, depending on where you are opening your restaurant.

You want to build a wine list that is user friendly. Your servers, bartenders, and staff will be the ones actually selling your wines, so it is important they feel comfortable with your menu. This means they need to be trained and understand the wine lists and have a feeling for what wines to recommend based on your restaurant menu. I have witnessed more than one server convince a guest to order a cocktail after the guest inquired about the difference between two cabernets. If your servers are pushing cocktails more than wine, they are also pushing labor-driven products. Your bartenders need to make cocktails, which typically takes longer than the two minutes it takes to pour a glass of wine. Selling wine can help your beverage sales and lead to more pleasant dining experiences for your guests.

Most restaurants do not have the luxury of opening with a wine list that has been developed by trial and error. While the majority of this book will be focused on how to design your menu, we will also briefly touch upon how to properly cost out your menu as well.

One of the biggest mistakes a restaurant can make is curating a wine list that is not made up of wines that sell in your local market but is made up of wines that the owner/employees enjoy drinking. This is an easy-to-make mistake, running a wine program has to be about current trends and tastes and, what is selling in your market. Of course, you should enjoy the wines on your menu, but they are there to make you money as well. Even if you are passionate about not including a chardonnay from Napa, it is possible your guests will be looking for an option like this and you want to make sure they have what they are looking for. For example, I had one regular guest who enjoyed wines from Hungary. I always had some wines for them on my list, because I knew they would become a frequent guest who wanted to showcase his favorite wine region to his guests.

Your wine list is also not a permanent fixture in your restaurant and it must have an organic, ever-changing menu. Wines will run out of stock, vineyard production will vary for a number of reasons, and price hikes will cause some products to be unobtainable. It is important to adjust your list accordingly and work with those who sell wine in your market to continue carrying an awesome wine list. As time goes on, you will want to adjust according to the demands of your guests as well. At one of my restaurants, I received a request almost every night for Moscato by the glass. After two months of this, I obliged and added it to the list, within a week the new wine outsold all my others. Listen to what your guests are asking for; their feedback is invaluable. I also like to have some wines for celebratory occasions on all of my menus, such as a champagne, but this might not apply to your venue.

Organization is key when running one or many different restaurants, and maintaining your costs is imperative for keeping your business successful. Ultimately, you are in charge of your beverage program, and this book is meant for guidance and suggestions.

Chapter 2
WHO I AM

Seeing as I will be assisting in curating your wine list, you may want to know a little about my qualifications. I have been running beverage programs for more than a decade. I have done everything from running wine lists with 1,100 selections that were awarded Wine Spectator's Best of Award of Excellence, to managing more than 18.7 million dollars of beverage sales per year at a restaurant group, overseeing multiple restaurants at once.

I am a Certified Sommelier through The Court of Master Sommeliers Americas and a Certified Specialist of Wine through the Society of Wine Educators. I am a Diploma student through the Wine and Spirits Education Trust. I have a Certified Sake Advisor certification through the Sake School of America, as well as an Executive Bourbon Steward certification through the Stake and Thief Society. My experience includes being a Sommelier at an internationally known luxury hotel, managing multiple profitable restaurants, and a Beverage Manager of a large restaurant group located in Pennsylvania and New Jersey.

Designing wine lists has always been a passion of mine,

How to Build a Wine List

and I regularly consult on new restaurants for their opening menus.

Chapter 3
KNOW YOUR MARKET

Markets can and will vary drastically. There are many reasons I cannot tell you to go out and plug a particular high end Chardonnay onto your menu. It may not be available in your market at all, the local price of it may be drastically different than what your market supports, or the distributor who carries it might have a ten-case minimum order on it, etc. But with that said there are many opportunities that present themselves when curating a wine list.

Templates are meant to be a guideline of what your menu should look like structurally. You also want your menu to be unique to your venue; otherwise it would not be special. You can honestly say you have an in-house curated wine list with this method. My best suggestion is to select a template that speaks to you. Before moving forward, you can add selections that you are passionate about and are missing, or remove wines that you dislike. Email your distributors (more than one) the list of what you are searching for, and ask them to bring in samples that fit the theme. Make some time and taste through them and take notes on your favorites.

Something else I highly recommend is checking out your competition. When I was building a wine menu in Nashville, I looked up all the neighboring restaurants and analyzed their lists. There was a remarkable amount of natural wines in their programs, including orange wines by the glass. Orange wines are made from green grape varietals but with the same process as red wines, i.e. the winemaker will crush the grapes and leave the juice in contact with the skins until tannin and color is introduced in the wine. These wines are orange in hue, but transparent like a rosé-style wine. After seeing this pattern, I decided to put an orange wine on the glass list of the new restaurant. It sold shockingly well.

If you are in a natural-loving wine market, you would do well to make sure you have your natural wines on the menu, including Pétillant-Naturel sparkling. Another restaurant I worked at had the average age bracket of guests 50+ who drank primarily Napa Cabernets. I needed to pivot the wine list accordingly and make sure there were enough selections of these wines for the opening. Use your competition to your advantage. Go in to eat and observe what people are ordering at the bar and drinking. Take a look at their menu and ask yourself why the wines they have are on there.

Also take a look at your own business model. If you are a fast casual restaurant, it would be great to have a smaller wine list with moderate pricing. If you are opening a fine-dining operation, you are going to need a larger list with more expensive selections. (does this have implications to the number of wines offered by the glass vs the bottle)? Perhaps you open in an area where guests love wine and do not mind spending money on a nice bottle. If that is the case, add to your list appropriately. I have worked in restaurants where we sold wines for four or even *five* figures, and guests did not seem shocked or surprised by it. If your market or restaurant concept can sell higher-end-bottles of wine, it would not hurt to have one or two bottles on hand to test the market. If you are beginning to dabble in the higher-end wine industry, I highly suggest hiring a Sommelier consultant or bringing on a full-time Sommelier to oversee your program. Fine dining traditionally has smaller profit margins than fast casual, and adjustments if not done carefully can have a negative impact on your margins.

With the templates listed in this book, I will explain all the selections, and you can decide what works best for your establishment.

Chapter 4
SELECTIONS AND SIZE

There are many different styles of wine lists and no right way to list your wines. Some lists have descriptions of all the wines, so guests can see what to expect from their wines. Some are arranged in style (lightest to heaviest or vice versa). I recommend making the menu as user-friendly as possible. You would also like your wine list to match the theme of your restaurant. In the wine world, there is a saying, "What grows together, goes together." If you are an Italian restaurant, you might want to have an Italian-focused wine list. If you were to have only French wines, your guests would be confused and might have a hard time selecting what to order.

If you are a fast casual restaurant, there would be no reason to have a wine list with 1,000 selections. Make sure your concept and your menu make sense together. Shorter lists can be as short as 10 wines. Longer lists can look like dictionaries and hold more than 5,000 selections. Make sure your style of list matches your intentions.

Designers can easily be hired to create a menu that matches your brand. For a faster and less expensive solution, there are many templates you can purchase online.

Chapter 5
SOMMELIERS

Sommeliers are always helpful to have on staff, as they are able to guide guests through the selection process. They are able to sell wines that might have sat unnoticed by guests. Sommelier certifications are offered through a variety of classes and examinations, some more prestigious than others. Whatever the level of Sommelier, they should be able to speak to guests about styles of wine and flavor profiles.

If you are unable to have a Sommelier on staff, it is helpful to list your menu in an understandable fashion. I like to organize mine by style, ranging from light to heavy. If you are able to have a tasting note for each wine, it does help guests pick which bottle they are most interested in.

In most states, your distributors are allowed to do training with your staff. I highly recommend utilizing this. Have your staff learn about each wine on your menu so they can answer questions your guests may have about them. There are few things that will impress your guest as much as a truly well-informed server. I suggest tasting at least one wine a week with them (if they are of legal drinking age) and keep them engaged in the wine menu.

Chapter 6
TEMPLATES WITH EXPLANATIONS

These templates are meant to be guides for building your wine lists. They should be tailored to your market and adjusted after opening to better suit your guests' wants and needs.

The wines with asterisks are my recommended wines by the glass.*

The price ranges are what the restaurant will be paying for the wine. Be sure to price it accordingly to keep your business profitable. I recommend a 24 percent cost of goods sold on your wines by the glass at a standard 5 oz pour. Your wines by the bottle can run at a higher cost of goods sold, closer to 28 percent. You should adjust however you see fit.

The easiest way to use these templates is to tell your local distributors these are the wines you are searching for and ask them to bring you samples. Taste the wines they bring, and select your favorite that fits into the parameters.

Chapter 7
CLASSICALLY INSPIRED WINE LIST TEMPLATE

30 Selections Wine List (Classically Inspired)

SPARKLING Wines—5 Selections
1. Inexpensive Sparkling for cocktails $3-6/bottle*
2. Prosecco $7-12/bottle*
3. Inexpensive Sparkling Rosé $10-16/bottle*
4. Champagne for casual nights $40-50/bottle
5. Celebratory Champagne $50-75/bottle

WHITE WINES–9 Selections
1. New Zealand Sauvignon Blanc $7-14/bottle*
2. Pinot Grigio from Italy $7-12/bottle*
3. French Chardonnay $8-12/bottle*
4. American Chardonnay $8-12/bottle*
5. Off-dry Riesling $8-12/bottle*
6. Sancerre $20-30/bottle

7. American Chardonnay $20-30/bottle
8. White Burgundy $20-30/bottle
9. Pinot Gris from Oregon $10-20/bottle

ROSÉ WINES–3 Selections
1. Provence Rosé $10-14/bottle*
2. American Rosé $10-12/bottle*
3. Higher End Rosé $15-25/bottle

RED WINES–12 Selections
1. Malbec from Argentina $10-14/bottle*
2. Tempranillo from Spain $10-16/bottle*
3. Pinot Noir from America $8-14/bottle*
4. Cabernet Sauvignon from America $8-14/bottle*
5. Zinfandel from America $8-12/bottle*
6. Sangiovese from Italy $12-20/bottle
7. Cabernet Sauvignon from America $20-30/bottle
8. Cabernet Sauvignon from America $30-40/bottle
9. Pinot Noir from Oregon $15-25/bottle
10. Pinot Noir from Burgundy $20-35/bottle
11. Bordeaux from France $20-30/bottle
12. Pinotage from South Africa $15-25/bottle

DESSERT WINE–1 Selection
1. Port Wine $12-25/bottle*

Sparkling wine selection involves five options. You need an inexpensive sparkling $3-6/bottle* to use for not only cocktails but also complementary toasts. I recommend gifting glasses of these, for anniversaries, long wait times at the door, and smoothing over guests who are upset over something. With prices as low as $3-6/bottle you will be spending anywhere from $0.60-1.20/glass on these events. This option may or may not be listed on the menu at your discretion. I have kept this wine off my lists and just had them on hand to use. The popularity of Prosecco will make this a strong recommendation, as people will ask for it by name. The price of $7-12/bottle* is a good range to make a good profit on it.

You are going to want to have an inexpensive sparkling rosé as well for the diversity of your bubbles. This will be a bigger hit in the warmer seasons, and with a price range of $10-16/bottle* you should be able to turn a good profit on them. Champagne for casual nights running $40-50/bottle is great from your everyday upselling. Celebratory Champagne coming in at $50-75/bottle is for when people are coming to your establishment to spend money. I recommend only having a few (two to three) bottles of this on hand, unless you are regularly selling more than anticipated.

The white wine selections include nine options that are prevalent in the market. New Zealand Sauvignon Blanc running around $7-14/bottle* is consistently in the top three most- popular pours at the majority of my restaurants. You are more than welcome to try a Sauvignon Blanc from other regions, but when I have deviated, guests were less than happy about it and requested one from New Zealand.

Another heavy hitter, Pinot Grigio from Italy around $7-12/bottle* is normally in the top five of my best-selling wines. I have plenty of typical guests who will ask for a Pinot Grigio to drink without even looking at the menu. A popular requested grape varietal is chardonnay, but there is more than one popular style. In this classic list I have one of each, with French Chardonnay $8-12/bottle* and an American Chardonnay $8-12/bottle.* The French Chardonnay is typically lighter and leaner in style and beloved by some. The

How to Build a Wine List

American style is richer with more texture and some buttery oak notes. When someone loves to drink chardonnay they will most likely know which style they prefer. It is good to have the two options, so you do not make one or the other guest settle for the style they do not enjoy.

For white wines, you will also need one with some sweetness to it. Listen to your guests and plan accordingly. I suggest an off-dry Riesling running from $8-12/bottle,* because the Riesling grape varietal is popular. This style has some sweetness but is not cloying or dessert-like. Some restaurants might prefer to have a Moscato by the glass, but these tend to be more dessert style. A higher-end Sauvignon Blanc is normally what I sell to guests who enjoy a nice crisp white wine but are happy with spending a bit more money. Sancerre is an extremely popular region in France, and I typically sell this bottle more than others with the cost of it for me running $20-30/bottle.

Running into that chardonnay problem again, I do like to have both styles available on a higher-end scale. American Chardonnay for $20-30/bottle and White Burgundy for $20-30/bottle tend to perform well on my lists for guests who are enjoying your wines by-the-glass selections, but would like higher quality than what is offered by the glass. This last selection is more flexible, and I highly recommend you check out the market around you for it. I suggest Pinot Gris from Oregon, running from $10-20/bottle, as it is a higher-end Pinot Grigio selection. These are typically the least sold on the menu.

Rosé wines are fun to select, but know you will not move much of them until the warmer seasons. Three selections include a Provence Rosé around $10-14/bottle,* an American Rosé at $10-12/bottle,* and a higher-end rosé from $15-25/bottle. The Provence style will most likely be the rosé most ordered and sought after. There are plenty of American rosés that are excellent, and at lower prices than those being imported from France. The third is a bottle only, as it is priced too high to sell by the glass. For this wine, you might want to choose a well-known brand that is sure to sell itself. There are plenty of higher priced rosé wines with notoriety to choose from.

Moving onto our 12 selections of red wines, I had Malbec from Argentina coming in around $10-14/bottle* to start. This classic wine is easily loveable at a great price. A classic Tempranillo from Spain from $10-16/bottle* might mean a Rioja style wine. These wines are spicy and complex, making for a wonderful drinking experience. A light and lean Pinot Noir from America for around $8-14/bottle* is up next. I loosely wrote from America, but Oregon is preferable to California, in my experience. There are plenty of amazing Pinot Noirs produced in California, but in my experience, the market seems to be demanding their counterparts from Oregon in the past few years. Save yourself the headache of redoing your list selection, and start off with one from Oregon.

A bold and juicy Cabernet Sauvignon from America for $8-14/bottle* is going to be one of your best sellers, and normally runs at the top of your Product Mix, or PMIX, reports. California is a great region to look around for this wine, as well as Washington. A Zinfandel from America around $8-12/bottle* is easy enough to recognize for your guests and will sell itself, especially with heavy meat dishes and BBQ. Moving onto our bottle selections, I recommend a Sangiovese from Italy around $12-20/bottle. These wines will most likely come from or around the region of Chianti in Tuscany. They are well paired with pizza and pasta dishes. A higher-end option for Cabernet Sauvignon from America at two price points, $20-30/bottle and $30-40/bottle. These wines will most likely be coming from California or Washington, just like your glass pour.

Two Pinot Noirs on the list for a higher-end selection than

How to Build a Wine List

your glass pour would be a Pinot Noir from Oregon around $15-25/bottle and a Pinot Noir from Burgundy in the $20-35/bottle range. These two are classic expressions of the grape varietal and a true lover of Pinot Noir will appreciate both of them. A lovely Bordeaux from France from $20-30/bottle will add a little more texture to your list. These wines are famous and at least one should be included in a classic wine list. We finish up our red selection with a classic Pinotage from South Africa for around $15-25/bottle. These wines are a cross between Pinot Noir and Cinsault and have really made a name for themselves in the past few years.

Our dessert-wine selection is a Port Wine from $12-25/bottle.* These wines hail from Portugal and are fortified dessert wines. They are typically served in two-ounce pours in Port glasses.

Chapter 8
FRENCH INSPIRED WINE LIST TEMPLATE

30 Selections Wine List (French Inspired)

SPARKLING Wines—5 Selections
1. Inexpensive Sparkling for cocktails $3-6/bottle*
2. Crémant Sparkling $7-12/bottle*
3. French Crémant Rosé $10-16/bottle*
4. Champagne for casual nights $40-50/bottle
5. Celebratory Champagne $50-75/bottle

WHITE WINES–9 Selections
1. Loire Valley Sauvignon Blanc $7-14/bottle*
2. Pinot Grigio from the Veneto $7-12/bottle*
3. French Chardonnay $8-12/bottle*
4. American Chardonnay $8-12/bottle*
5. Off-dry Chenin Blanc $8-12/bottle*
6. Sancerre $20-30/bottle

7. American Chardonnay $20-30/bottle
8. White Burgundy $20-30/bottle
9. Pinot Gris from Alsace $10-20/bottle

ROSÉ WINES–3 Selections
1. Provence Rosé $10-14/bottle*
2. Languedoc Rosé $10-12/bottle*
3. Higher-End French Rosé $15-25/bottle

RED WINES–12 Selections
1. Malbec from Cahors $10-14/bottle*
2. Cabernet from America or Loire $10-16/bottle*
3. Pinot Noir from Burgundy $8-14/bottle*
4. Cabernet from Bordeaux $8-14/bottle*
5. Merlot from Bordeaux $8-12/bottle*
6. Côte du Rhône from Rhône $12-20/bottle
7. Cabernet from America or Bordeaux $20-30/bottle
8. Cabernet from America $30-40/bottle
9. Pinot Noir from Oregon $15-25/bottle
10. Pinot Noir from Burgundy $20-35/bottle
11. Châteauneuf-du-Pape from Rhône Valley $25-40/bottle
12. Merlot from America or France $15-20/bottle

DESSERT WINE–1 Selection
1. Pineau des Charentes $12-25/bottle*

I recommend five selections of sparkling wines for your list. You will need an inexpensive sparkling for cocktails ranging from $3-6/bottle.* This wine will be used in cocktails, as well as for complementary occasions such as an anniversary. If you have guests who are upset with long wait times or want to make their meal special, you can give away this wine, and it would only cost you $0.60-1.20/glass.

A crémant sparkling $7-12/bottle* is a wine made in the same method as Champagne, but it is produced in a different region. These are normally value-driven wines. You will also want to have a crémant rosé $10-16/bottle,* so those who are looking for pink bubbles will not be disappointed. Champagne for casual nights at $40-50/bottle includes brands that are easy to recognize, such as Veuve Clicquot. These brand-driven wines sell themselves on a wine list. I like to have Celebratory Champagne from $50-75/bottle on my lists in case someone is celebrating a special occasion and would like to spend a bit more money.

For our white wines, we should stay around the nine-selections mark. Sauvignon Blanc is a popular variety, and arguably some of the best known ones come from Loire Valley. There are other regions you could explore with these crisp and refreshing wines, such as Bordeaux, but Loire will be the easiest to recognize. The price range of $7-14/bottle is ideal for optimizing profits, while maintaining high quality. Pinot Grigio from the Veneto is consistently one of my best-selling wines on lists. You are more than welcome to look for another French wine that fits in this slot, but if your guests keep requesting a Pinot Grigio, I recommend yielding to them. The price tag of $7-12/bottle is reasonable for a good bottle of this easy-drinking wine.

Chardonnay is a polarizing grape and some people really love one style over the other. We take that into account by pouring a French Chardonnay as well as an American Chardonnay. I recommend having one French Chardonnay, ranging from $8-12/bottle,* as well as one American Chardonnay, ranging from $8-12/bottle.* This

How to Build a Wine List

way you are not ignoring one side of the chardonnay-loving guests.

We also need a sweet option on the list for those who will ask. I suggest having an off-dry Chenin Blanc from Loire Valley from $8-12/bottle.* This wine is refreshing and a real crowd pleaser, while filling that gap for guests who want a little more sweetness. Sancerre is a vastly popular higher-end Sauvignon Blanc that you should aim for, at around $20-30/bottle. These wines go well with lighter fare. Similarly with the Chardonnay conundrum for by the glass, having a higher-end American Chardonnay at $20-30/bottle and a white Burgundy at $20-30/bottle is an excellent addition to the wine list. The last wine I recommend is a wine from Alsace. My selection would be a Pinot Gris from Alsace, hugging around $10-20/bottle.

Red wine selections should encompass about twelve different selections. Malbec is growing in popularity as a grape varietal, and France makes some lovely ones at lower price points. Malbec from Cahors, ranging from $10-14/bottle,* is my recommendation. For by the glass, I suggest a Cabernet Franc from America or Loire Valley, around $10-16/bottle.* Cabernet Franc from America can have an easily recognizable location for your guests to grab onto. Cabernet Franc from Loire Valley tends to be more on theme of the list, but can be a little leaner and lighter than Cabernet from America. A classic wine that French Oenophiles look for is a Pinot Noir from Burgundy by the glass, which will require a price point of $8-14/bottle.* These lighter-in-style wines pair with a wide array of foods, and guests will keep an eye out for them.

Moving into some heavier-styled wines, I also recommend a Cabernet Sauvignon or Cabernet Sauvignon Blend from Bordeaux. Both this grape and the region are easy to recognize and will bring comfort to a guest looking for a wine of this style. Cabernet from Bordeaux, coming in around $8-14/bottle,* should be easy enough to find and a real popular menu item. Hailing most likely from the opposite bank in Bordeaux, a Merlot from Bordeaux ranging $8-12/bottle* is my recommendation. These wines are softer and more plush than the Cabernets from Bordeaux, but a lot of value is packed into them. Merlot is a familiar enough grape varietal that a guest will gravitate toward it.

For some additional bottle selections, I suggest a Côte du Rhône from Rhône Valley around $12-20/bottle, your cost. These wines are typically blends of multiple grapes including Grenache, Syrah, and Mourvèdre. They typically are fruit-driven and pair exceptionally well with game and meat. If you have a French wine lover, there is a good chance they are familiar with these wines. For higher-end selections that will end up at a sweet point for pricing on your list, I recommend a Cabernet Sauvignon from America or Bordeaux around $20-30/bottle, as well as a Cabernet from America coming in at $30-40/bottle. These higher-end options will come out to a good price point for those having business meetings or splurging.

Another area of the list should include some Pinot Noir from Oregon, around $15-25/bottle, as well as a Pinot Noir from Burgundy from $20-35/bottle. These lighter styles are really needed for your light dishes and guests who only enjoy light-red wines. A real crowd pleaser is a Châteauneuf-du-Pape from Rhône Valley from $25-40/bottle. These wines are also from the Rhône and encompass a blend of up to thirteen grapes, including Grenache, Mourvèdre, Syrah, and Cinsault grapes. To finish off our reds, I suggest a Merlot from America or France at around $15-20/bottle. Plushy and approachable, it is a little higher-end than what is offered by the glass. For dessert, a lovely Pineau des Charentes from $12-25/bottle* would round off this list nicely.

Chapter 9
ITALIAN INSPIRED WINE LIST TEMPLATE

30 Selections Wine List (Italian Inspired)

SPARKLING Wines—5 Selections
1. Inexpensive Sparkling for cocktails $3-6/bottle*
2. Prosecco $7-12/bottle*
3. Prosecco Rosé $10-16/bottle*
4. Lambrusco $20-40/bottle
5. Celebratory Franciacorta $50-75/bottle

WHITE WINES–9 Selections
1. Friuli-Venezia Giulia or Veneto Sauvignon Blanc $7-14/bottle*
2. Pinot Grigio from Veneto $7-12/bottle*
3. Italian Chardonnay $8-12/bottle*
4. Cortese from Piedmont $8-12/bottle*
5. Moscato from Piedmont $8-12/bottle*
6. Falanghina from Campania $20-30/bottle
7. American Chardonnay $20-30/bottle

8. White Burgundy $20-30/bottle
9. Fiano from Campania $10-20/bottle

ROSÉ WINES–3 Selections
1. Provence Rosé $10-14/bottle*
2. Italian Rosé $10-12/bottle*
3. Higher End Italian Rosé $15-25/bottle

RED WINES–12 Selections
1. Sangiovese from Tuscany $10-14/bottle*
2. Cabernet from America or Tuscany $10-16/bottle*
3. Montepulciano from Abruzzo $8-14/bottle*
4. Nebbiolo from Piedmont $8-16/bottle*
5. Barbera from Piedmont $8-12/bottle*
6. Aglianico from Campania or Basilicata $25-35/bottle
7. Cabernet from America or Bordeaux $20-30/bottle
8. Cabernet from America $30-40/bottle
9. Pinot Noir from Oregon $15-25/bottle
10. Super Tuscan Blend from Tuscany $20-35/bottle
11. Barolo or Barbaresco from Piedmont $25-40/bottle
12. Nero d'Avola from Sicily $15-20/bottle

DESSERT WINE–1 Selection
1. Vin Santo from Montepulciano $12-25/bottle*

How to Build a Wine List

For our Italian inspired wine list I suggest five sparkling wines. You will still need an inexpensive bottle of bubbles for cocktails and complementary occasions. To have a bottle in the $3-6 price range will save you from pouring a more-expensive glass. It should cost anywhere from $0.59-1.18/glass, which is well worth making a guest happy. Prosecco has gained popularity to the point of reaching more expensive prices now, but it does hail from Italy. The rosé style of Prosecco will make an excellent addition to your sparkling wines. These blush glasses tend to sell in the warmer seasons. An underrated sparkling wine coming from Italy is Lambrusco, which varies in sweetness levels, and is red in color. This wine is growing in popularity in some markets such as New York. A higher-end option is always important for your guests who are celebrating, and Franciacorta is my selection for them. This wine is made in the same method as Champagne, but originates from the Lombardi region of Italy.

White wines I chose nine selections. Friuli-Venezia Giulia or Veneto Sauvignon Blanc coming in around $7-14/bottle* will be one of your top sellers. These wines are universally loved and pair exceptionally well with seafood due to their minerality. Another heavy hitter on any wine list will be a Pinot Grigio from Veneto ranging $7-12/bottle.* This wine is often one ordered without so much as a glance at the brand. So beloved is Pinot Grigio from Italy, I often put it on wine lists inspired by other regions in the world. Italian Chardonnay from $8-12/bottle* adds a splash of uniqueness to your list. Chardonnay from Italy can vary drastically in style, so make sure to taste around for your favorite. This grape would surely attract attention if it was missing. Cortese from Piedmont ranging from $8-12/bottle* brings a light crisp wine with lots of citrus notes to it. It is easy-drinking enough to charm anyone who is wary of trying a new wine.

To finish up our glass pours, we need something with some sweetness. Moscato from Piedmont from $8-12/bottle* will be sought after in some markets even more than a white zinfandel would be. I highly recommend stacking your list with one of these floral and lightly sparkling wines. For a white wine with a little more texture and richness that can stand up to heavier fish dishes, Falanghina from Campania, coming in at around $20-30/bottle, hits the mark. Some of your guests might not recognize this grape, but others will be delighted to find it here. American Chardonnay is a classic wine that will be missed if it is not on your list. Having an example of a French Chardonnay would not hurt this list, which is why I choose a White Burgundy in the same price point of $20-30/bottle. The last wine I selected is a Fiano from Campania from $10-20/bottle. This is an excellent wine for Italian white wine lovers to try if they are unfamiliar, as it does pair nicely with the cuisine.

Even though this list is Italian inspired, I do suggest to keep a Provence Rosé from $10-14/bottle.* These wines are sought after enough that guests will request it if it is not there. The next two rosé wines are Italian. For the glass program, a nice Italian Rosé from $10-12/bottle* will complement your food nicely. These wines vary depending on where they come from, but some made from the Sangiovese grape varietal are my personal favorite. Also, get one higher-end Italian rosé around $15-25/bottle for those who want to upgrade their selection for the night. Stocking-wise, I would not have more than two to three bottles on hand, unless it sells better than expected.

Red wines from Italy are varied and excellent. Your guests will be happy to choose Italian wines to pair with their meals. For a lighter-bodied red wine, the Sangiovese from Tuscany, coming in around $10-14/bottle,* hits the mark. This grape is native to the region, and all those who grew up drinking Chianti will be happy to see it here. For a classic variety, we have a Cabernet Sauvignon from America or Tuscany coming in at $10-16/bottle.* This grape is grown globally, and some fine expressions of it are made in Tuscany. Pick one that represents your brand the best.

For something fruity and easy-drinking, a Montepulciano from Abruzzo, ranging from $8-14/bottle,* will suffice. This wine is delightful and easy-drinking for those who ask for a red wine that is not so dry. My tannin-heavy selection is a Nebbiolo from Piedmont, coming in around $8-16/bottle.* These wines are translucent like Pinot Noir, but they pack a powerful tannic punch. They are excellent with heavier fare and especially tomatoes. The last by-the-glass selection is a Barbera from Piedmont from $8-12/bottle.* This iconic grape varietal is a crowd pleaser, and guests will be torn between this and the Montepulciano.

Moving into our bottle selections, Aglianico from Campania or Basilicata, ranging from $25-35/bottle, is an excellent addition to the list. This wine is *extremely* big and bold with aggressive tannin. It pairs exceptionally well with rich meat dishes, and guests who ask for a big wine are not disappointed with this selection. A classic Cabernet Sauvignon from America or Bordeaux at around $20-30/bottle is always a good option to have available, as they do tend to sell easily. A higher-end version of that with a Cabernet Sauvignon from America from $30-40/bottle will allow guests who are happy to spend more money do so. A light and lean Pinot Noir from Oregon for $15-25/bottle will add another layer of depth to your wine list and make your Pinot fans happy. Another big and bold selection is a Super Tuscan Blend from Tuscany around $20-35/bottle. This wine is made from some combination of Bordeaux grape varietals (Cabernet Sauvignon, Cabernet Franc, Merlot, etc.), and sometimes Sangiovese.

The last two suggestions include a Barolo or Barbaresco from Piedmont for $25-40/bottle. Barolo is known as the King and Barbaresco the Queen of Piedmont. These wines are both made from Nebbiolo, but come from different regions and are aged differently. These wines are elegant to the extreme and highly sought after. A more light-hearted selection is our last red, a Nero d'Avola from Sicily for around $15-20/bottle. This wine is well known, but if you are looking for an alternative, I suggest trying a Nerello Mascalese. Both are sure to round out your wine list. For a sweet finish, I recommend a Vin Santo from Montepulciano for $12-25/bottle.* These wines are sticky and lusciously sweet and sure to be a perfect pairing with some biscotti at the end of a meal.

Chapter 10
ASIAN INSPIRED WINE LIST TEMPLATE

30 Selections Wine List (Asian Inspired)

SPARKLING Wines—7 Selections
1. Inexpensive Sparkling for cocktails $3-6/bottle*
2. Prosecco $7-12/bottle*
3. Rosé $10-16/bottle*
4. Sparkling AWA Sake $10-20/bottle
5. Lambrusco $20-40/bottle
6. Champagne for casual nights $40-50/bottle
7. Celebratory Champagne $50-75/bottle

WHITE WINES–10 Selections
1. New Zealand Sauvignon Blanc $7-14/bottle*
2. Pinot Grigio from Veneto $7-12/bottle*
3. French Chardonnay $8-12/bottle*
4. Ginjo Sake $8-14/bottle*

5. Junmai Sake $8-14/bottle*
6. Off-dry Riesling $8-12/bottle*
7. American Chardonnay $20-30/bottle
8. White Burgundy $20-30/bottle
9. Gewürztraminer from Alsace or America $10-20/bottle
10. Sancerre $20-30/bottle

ROSÉ WINES–3 Selections
1. Provence Rosé $10-14/bottle*
2. American Rosé $10-12/bottle*
3. Rosé Sake $15-25/bottle

RED WINES–9 Selections
1. Sangiovese from Tuscany $10-14/bottle*
2. Cabernet Sauvignon from America $10-16/bottle*
3. Pinot Noir from Oregon $8-14/bottle*
4. Merlot from America $8-16/bottle*
5. Malbec from France or Argentina $8-12/bottle*
6. Cabernet from America or Bordeaux $20-30/bottle
7. Cabernet from America $30-40/bottle
8. Pinot Noir from Oregon $15-25/bottle
9. Zinfandel from America $15-25/bottle

DESSERT WINE–1 Selection
1. Moscato from Italy $8-12/bottle*

"Asian inspired" sounds a little broad, and it is. I am not discounting that this continent is vast and there are many different cuisines that call Asia home. Rather than work on specifics, I thought keeping it broad would allow for more flexibility for you. These cuisines tend to be extremely flavorful and lighter with more vegetables. Because of this we are working toward a menu that is lighter in style and complements the food.

For our sparkling wines I decided on seven selections. The classic inexpensive sparkling for cocktails and complementary use ranges from $3-6/bottle.* This wine might not be listed on your menu but will greatly help in keeping costs down for your cocktails and guest attentiveness. Next we have a Prosecco ranging from $7-12/bottle.* Your guests will ask for this wine by name. A sparkling rosé around $10-16/bottle* is always a welcome addition to a menu. There are so many regions that make these, it should be easy to find.

Continuing with our light and refreshing sparkling wines, we have a sparkling AWA Sake from $10-20/bottle. This wine is made from rice and has been said to pair better with food than grape wines do, due to the acids in it. Whichever wine you are passionate about, it does not hurt to add one of these to your selection. A nice red Lambrusco from Italy coming in around $20-40/bottle adds a nice touch for those looking for a sparkling red wine to pair with their food. Two price points of champagne round out this sparkling selection: one for casual nights at around $40-50/bottle and one for celebrations at around $50-75/bottle. You don't need to have much of these in stock, but they are incredibly helpful to have if someone is looking for them.

With our cuisines being more white-wine friendly, this list has ten selections of whites. The classic and beloved New Zealand Sauvignon Blanc for around $7-14/bottle* is a sought after wine you will be sorry not to have listed. Another popular wine is our Pinot Grigio from Italy around $7-12/bottle*. This wine will sell itself, and it will sell a lot. A light and crisp French Chardonnay around $8-12/bottle* will make your chardonnay lovers happy. Two styles of Sake for the glass pours I recommend are Ginjo and Junmai. I did list the other styles for you, and it is perfectly okay to deviate from this list. Try to find both in the $8-14/bottle* price range. Depending on how spicy your menu is, you might want to have more than one off-dry selection. For this template, however, I selected an off-dry Riesling at the $8-12/bottle* price. If you have very heavily seasoned or spiced dishes, you might want to add another off-dry selection, and I would choose a Chenin Blanc.

For our chardonnay fans, we do have two higher-end options available for the bottle selection. American Chardonnay for $20-30/bottle and a White Burgundy for $20-30/bottle. These wines are very different in style, but if someone is a fan of the varietal, they know which they prefer. The French (White Burgundy) is going to be mineral and crisp, while the American will boast a creamy texture and some oak and spice notes. A fun selection for an Asian-inspired menu is a Gewürztraminer from Alsace or America around $10-20/bottle. This floral wine smells like potpourri and can stand up to well-seasoned dishes. The final selection is a higher-end Sauvignon Blanc from France, a Sancerre from $20-30/bottle. These ten whites will make a great base to your menu.

For rosé I am sticking with three recommendations. A Provence Rosé at $10-14/bottle* will always have guests asking for it. It is the region that brought fame and glory to the pink wine we all know and love and has earned its spot on the list. An American Rosé around $10-12/bottle* is my suggestion for another glass pour that could be a vast variety of grapes or regions. It is on this menu for those who are biased toward American wines. Finally, we round it out with a Rosé Sake around $15-25/bottle. This sake typically gets its beautiful pink coloring from a red yeast during the fermentation process. Some of these wines have some sweetness to them, so be sure to try before selecting one.

Going a little lighter on our red wines, I chose nine selections for this themed wine list. The first is a light and lean Sangiovese from Tuscany coming in around $10-14/bottle.* This wine has some green notes as well as tomato normally on the palate that should complement the food nicely. A heavier Cabernet Sauvignon from America around $10-16/bottle* might not pair with all of the food on your menu, but it will be sought after as a crowd favorite for your bottle sales. A nice light Pinot Noir from Oregon around $8-14/bottle* will pair beautifully with highly seasoned or lightly spiced foods. A common grape, Merlot from America around $8-16/bottle,* will make an excellent addition, but it might be the least sold wine on your menu. Keep an eye on this one and remove it if you think it is a waste of space.

Gaining popularity, a Malbec from France or Argentina, coming in around $8-12/bottle,* is an easy crowd pleaser. Although this grape is fairly well known, it is still less recognizable than the most popular grapes. Speaking of popular grapes, next we have a Cabernet Sauvignon from America or Bordeaux from $20-30/bottle as well as the same grape at $30-40/bottle. Another classic that will pair well with lighter fare is our Pinot Noir from Oregon at $15-25/bottle. You could replace this with a nice Pinot from Burgundy if you prefer, but having a bottle of this grape is a must. Lastly we have a Zinfandel from America, coming in around $15-25/bottle. Some jamminess and spice will finish off the red selections. For a dessert wine, I chose Moscato from Italy at $8-12/bottle,* because it is light and refreshing and not too sticky or thick.

SOME SAKE STYLES and Their Meanings

- **JUNMAI DAIGINJO:** highest-quality sake, rice polish 50% or more, no alcohol added
- **DAIGINGO:** brewed with very highly polished rice, artisanal, delicious, the pinnacle of the brewer's art
- **JUNMAI GINJO:** high-quality sake, rice polish 60% or more, no alcohol added
- **GINJO:** rice polish 50% of original size, small amount of pure distilled alcohol added
- **TOKUBETSU JUNMAI:** special, rice polish 60% of original size, no alcohol added
- **UNMAI:** rice polish 70% of original size, no alcohol added
- **HONJOZO:** small amount of pure distilled alcohol is added
- **NIGORI:** sparkling OR still unfiltered sake
- **AWA:** sparkling sake

Chapter 11
NORTH AMERICAN INSPIRED WINE LIST TEMPLATE

30 Selections Wine List (North American Inspired)

SPARKLING Wines—5 Selection
1. Inexpensive Sparkling for cocktails $3-6/bottle*
2. American Sparkling $7-12/bottle*
3. American Sparkling Rosé $10-16/bottle*
4. Champagne for casual nights $40-50/bottle
5. Celebratory Champagne $50-75/bottle

WHITE WINES–9 Selections
1. California or New York Sauvignon Blanc $7-14/bottle*
2. Pinot Grigio/Gris from America $7-12/bottle*
3. White Zinfandel $8-12/bottle*
4. American Chardonnay $8-12/bottle*
5. Dry Riesling from New York State

$8-12/bottle*
6. American Viognier $20-25/bottle
7. American Chardonnay $20-30/bottle
8. Pinot Blanc from America $20-30/bottle
9. Gruner Veltliner from America $10-20/bottle

ROSÉ WINES—3 Selections
1. Provence Rosé $10-14/bottle*
2. American Rosé $10-12/bottle*
3. Higher End Rosé from Canada $15-25/bottle

RED WINES—12 Selections
1. Malbec from America $10-14/bottle*
2. Zinfandel from California $10-16/bottle*
3. Pinot Noir from Oregon $8-14/bottle*
4. Cabernet Sauvignon from California $8-14/bottle*
5. Grenache (or Blend) from America $8-12/bottle*
6. Merlot from California $12-20/bottle
7. Cabernet Sauvignon from California or Washington $20-30/bottle
8. Cabernet Sauvignon from California $30-40/bottle
9. Pinot Noir from Oregon $15-25/bottle
10. Pinot Noir from Oregon $25-35/bottle
11. Syrah from America $20-30/bottle
12. Grenache from America $15-20/bottle

DESSERT WINE—1 Selection

How to Build a Wine List

1. Ice Wine from Canada $20-45/bottle*

North America has some lovely options for wine. While not mentioned on this list, there are also extremely nice wines being made in Mexico if you are fortunate enough to get your hands on them. I suggest getting some of their Nebbiolo or Grenache. For sparkling selections I choose five wines to start with. An inexpensive sparkling for cocktails from $3-6/bottle* is always is good to have on your menu. An American Sparkling for $7-12/bottle* should be easy enough to find. There are plenty of sparkling wines coming out of New York state, Canada, Oregon, California, and more. See what is available in your region and choose what you believe to be the best. An American Sparkling Rosé at around $10-16/bottle* is also always helpful. These flush wines sell during spring and summer more frequently. I do suggest carrying two classic champagnes, even if they are not from North America. I would choose a name brand that is easily recognizable, as well as a grower champagne that might be more expensive. Prices ranging from $40-50/bottle and $50-75/bottle are excellent price points to use.

For white wines I choose nine major selections to start off with. A big hitter will be California or New York Sauvignon Blanc around $7-14/bottle.* These wines will be more tropical and less green than those coming from New Zealand. I recommend choosing a Sauvignon Blanc from these regions that tastes very citrusy, or you run the risk of your New Zealand lovers not enjoying them. I ran a domestic-only (American) wine list for a while, and guests constantly complained about the Sauvignon Blanc not being citrusy enough. California and New York Sauvignon Blancs can sometimes get too ripe, so keep a careful eye out for this. Having a Pinot Grigio/Gris from America around $7-12/bottle* will be extremely popular on your list as well. Oregon and Washington do a good job with this grape, and California will occasionally put forth some Pinot Grigio. Pinot Gris is actually the same grape as Pinot Grigio, but they are stylistically different. Pinot Grigio tends to be more fruit forward and sees only stainless steel in the aging process, while Pinot Gris is often aged for a short time in neutral barrels and is more mineral driven.

For an "off-dry" or sweeter selection, I chose a White Zinfandel around $8-12/bottle.* This wine is vastly popular in the United States and will be easily recognized. An American Chardonnay for around $8-12/bottle* is my next choice. While these wines can be oaky and buttery, your guests should be expecting that with an American-style chardonnay. For your last glass pour, I would choose a dry Riesling from New York State for around $8-12/bottle*. Draw attention to the fact that this is a dry wine on the menu itself, so guests do not confuse it with a sweet selection. These wines typically have searing minerality and are complex and layered. A wine list always benefits from having a dry Riesling, which is especially popular with Sauvignon Blanc drinkers.

For bottle selections we have some interesting grape varietals. An American Viognier for $20-25/bottle is always a welcome addition to a list. These grapes do well in warmer climates, so look for regions such as California, Virginia, Texas, and Arizona. An elevated American Chardonnay for $20-30/bottle will be hitting a sweet spot on your wine list for those looking for an upgrade from your glass pour. A Pinot Blanc from America at around $20-30/bottle would most likely be sourced from Oregon in the Willamette region, but some outliers grow them in Washington state and California as well. In Washington, check for the Columbia Valley region for some luscious expressions. Last for the white bottles is a Gruner Veltliner from America at around $10-20/bottle. This grape originated in Germany, but has been growing in popularity, and beautiful expressions of it can be found in Oregon and New York state. .

How to Build a Wine List

For our delicate pink wines, I recommend having three selections. A Provence Rosé for $10-14/bottle* is never out of place on any wine list. This classic region will be asked for even if you have a domestic-only wine list. The guests will inquire about it, so it is worth sticking on the list. An American Rosé around $10-12/bottle* could really come from any region in North America and could be made up of dozens of grapes. This is really personal preference as well as availability in your region. Less popular will be a higher-end rosé from Canada for around $15-25/bottle. You could choose one from America or Mexico as well, but Canada does have some stunning rosé wines made from Pinot Noir primarily and in this price range.

For red wines, we have twelve selections. A Malbec from America coming in around $10-14/bottle* is an excellent addition to the wine list. California, Washington, and Oregon have some lovely examples. A very American grape, Zinfandel from California, from $10-16/bottle,* is a beloved selection. For this version I recommend a bold and dry style. Pinot Noir from Oregon for a glass pour around $8-14/bottle* is going to be extremely popular for light-red-wine drinkers. You could also select a Pinot Noir from California, but it might be a little heavier in style, and your guests will ask about Oregon specifically. A nice bold Cabernet from California around $8-14/bottle* will be your top five best-selling wines, as it is consistently one of my top three wines. Make sure to choose one you can get plenty of. Consider a Grenache (or Blend) from America for $8-12/bottle.* I like some of the Grenache blends coming out of California these days (Paso Robles is making some excellent ones), but if you want to have a red blend that is not Grenache based, that is okay too. Check out your market and see what the demand is for.

For wines by the bottle, I started with a Merlot from California in the $12-20/bottle range. Since a certain movie came out bashing Merlot in 2004, the demand has never fully recovered for this classic grape. Those who love Merlot will seek it out though, and it is worth having on the menu. A nice juicy Cabernet Sauvignon from California or Washington for $20-30/bottle will be easy enough to find. The market is oversaturated with wines exactly like this at the moment. Pick your favorite from a distributor you enjoy working with and don't settle for a bottle you do not love, as there are so many to choose from. Also add a higher-end option of Cabernet Sauvignon from California or Washington, at around $30-40/bottle. This bottle will not sell as frequently as some others, but it is always good to have a bottle or two on hand in case someone is wanting to splurge. A bold and dramatic addition to your wine list is a Syrah from America for around $20-30/bottle. These meaty wines are grown in the warmer regions of America, with some excellent expressions coming from Mexico, California, and Arizona.

Lighter-in-style wines such as our Pinot Noir from Oregon, at around $15-25/bottle, help greatly for a fast-selling wine. Pinot Noirs tend to be lean, and they pair well with a wide array of foods, making these bottles of wine excellent for a party of three or four guests who ordered a variety of dishes, but wish to share one bottle of wine to pair. A slightly elevated option would not hurt, which is why we also have a Pinot Noir from Oregon in the $25-35/bottle price point. A fun way to finish up the red bottles is with a Grenache from America for around $15-20/bottle. If you can get your hands on an expression from Mexico, some great wines coming out of Valle de Guadalupe. Not one to skip dessert, I selected a fabulous Ice Wine from Canada from $20-45/bottle,* an epic way to finish your list.

Chapter 12
SOUTH AMERICAN INSPIRED WINE LIST TEMPLATE

30 Selections Wine List (South American Inspired)

SPARKLING Wines—5 Selection
1. Inexpensive Sparkling for cocktails $3-6/bottle*
2. Argentina Sparkling $7-12/bottle*
3. Brazil Sparkling Rosé $10-16/bottle*
4. Champagne method for casual nights $40-50/bottle
5. Celebratory Champagne method $50-75/bottle

WHITE WINES–9 Selections
1. Torrontés from Argentina $7-14/bottle*
2. Sauvignon Blanc $7-12/bottle*
3. Chardonnay from Argentina or Brazil $8-12/bottle*
4. Albariño from Uruguay or Argentina $8-12/bottle*

5. Riesling from Argentina or Chile $8-12/bottle*
6. Viognier from Argentina or Chile $20-25/bottle
7. Brazilian Chardonnay $20-30/bottle
8. Albariño from Uruguay $20-30/bottle
9. White Blends from Chile $10-20/bottle

ROSÉ WINES—3 Selections
1. Chilean Rosé $10-14/bottle*
2. Argentina Rosé $10-12/bottle*
3. Higher End Rosé from Brazil $15-25/bottle

RED WINES—12 Selections
1. Malbec from Argentina $10-14/bottle*
2. Carmenere from Chile $10-16/bottle*
3. Pinot Noir from Chile's Casablanca Valley or Argentina's Patagonia $8-14/bottle*
4. Cabernet Sauvignon from Chile, Argentina, or Brazil $8-14/bottle*
5. Syrah/Shiraz from Chile $8-12/bottle*
6. Merlot from Uruguay or Chile $12-20/bottle
7. Cabernet Sauvignon from Chile, Argentina, or Brazil $20-30/bottle
8. Cabernet Franc from Chile, Argentina, or Brazil $25-30/bottle
9. Petit Verdot from Chile $15-25/bottle
10. Pinot Noir from Chile's Casablanca Valley or Argentina's Patagonia $25-35/bottle
11. Bonarda from Argentina $20-30/bottle
12. Sangiovese from Argentina $15-20/bottle

How to Build a Wine List

. . .

DESSERT WINE–1 Selection
1. Late Harvest from Argentina
$20-45/bottle*

So many awesome wines are produced in South America, finding some should be easy enough, no matter which market you are working in. For sparkling wines, there is no shortage of production from South America. A good inexpensive sparkling for cocktails around $3-6/bottle* is necessary for keeping your costs down. This wine will not be winning any awards, but it has its place and purpose. A lovely Argentina Sparkling for $7-12/bottle* will make an excellent glass pour. For the other sparkling pour, a Brazilian Sparkling Rosé around $10-16/bottle* will add that splash of pink to the sparkling lineup. I do suggest having two higher-end options at the $40-50/bottle and $50-75/bottle price points. It does not matter which region it comes from, but it should be a true Champagne method. One at the lower price for casual nights, and one for special occasions at the higher price.

Our white wine selections are made up of nine that stand out in a lineup. The first is a Torrontés from Argentina for $7-14/bottle.* This aromatic wine is sure to please your guests looking for easy-drinking white wines. I also chose a Sauvignon Blanc for $7-12/bottle,* but I did not specify where to find this wine, as excellent expressions are made in almost every country in South America. See what your distributor has available, and taste through them to find your best option. A lovely chardonnay from Argentina or Brazil at around $8-12/bottle* will most likely be the heaviest in style of your white wines by the glass. You will absolutely need to try these before picking one, as they do vary drastically in style from buttery and creamy to crisp and refreshing.

Another popular grape is Albariño from Uruguay or

Argentina, ranging from $8-12/bottle.* This grape is better known today than a decade ago, and it is sure to have people ordering it confidently. Finishing off with a slightly sweet wine, I recommend pouring by the glass an off-dry Riesling from Argentina or Chile at $8-12/bottle.*

Moving onto our wine by the bottle, a great Viognier from Argentina or Chile, coming in around $20-25/bottle, will most likely not sell as frequently as the others, but when your guests try it, it is sure to leave them happy. A higher-end Brazilian Chardonnay from a $20-30/bottle range pairs beautifully with fish dishes. A higher-end Albariño from Uruguay around $20-30/bottle and a White Blend from Chile with $10-20/bottle round out the selection nicely.

There are a lot of rosé wines on the market, so finding these three suggested selections should be easy enough. A Chilean Rosé, ranging from $10-14/bottle,* can be made from a variety of grapes, but select one based on the flavor-profile you prefer. An Argentinian Rosé for $10-12/bottle* is another end-of-the-glass rosé pours. I recommend having them vary in color or style enough that when a guest asks which one is "more dry" or which is "lighter," your staff can effectively answer. A nice higher-end rosé from Brazil, coming in around $15-25/bottle, is a nice touch, although don't expect to sell much of this until the warmer months.

Jumping over to red wines, I chose twelve selections. A classic Malbec from Argentina at around $10-14/bottle* will be sought after by most of your guests. A Carménère from Chile, ranging from $10-16/bottle,* might not be as easily recognized, but the tannin structure and green notes are sure to win over your guests. I also chose a leaner Pinot Noir from Chile's Casablanca Valley or Argentina's Patagonia at around $8-14/bottle.* You will need that lean-and-easy-to-drink style of Pinot Noir for your lighter dishes. I singled out these two regions because they make wonderful examples of Pinot Noir, but if you find it elsewhere in your market, stick to that.

A Cabernet Sauvignon from Chile, Argentina, or Brazil for $8-14/bottle* is up next. You will need a Cabernet Sauvignon on your glass list, and there is a plethora of great wines coming from multiple regions in Chile, Argentina, and Brazil. Taste through some samples to find your favorite. Finishing up the glass list is a Syrah/Shiraz from Chile at $8-12/bottle.* Syrah and Shiraz are the same grape varietal, but they are typically named one way or the other, based on the style. The Syrahs of the world tend to run a little more earthy and lean than the Shirazes, which are fruity and jammy. Chile has some Syrah/Shiraz that you and your guests can fall in love with, with meatiness and structure to hold up to your heavier dishes.

Moving into our by-the-bottle selection, we have a Merlot from Uruguay or Chile at around $12-20/bottle. This wine is easily recognized and plushy enough to stand up to some meaty dishes. A higher-end Cabernet Sauvignon from Chile, Argentina, or Brazil is a must, coming in around $20-30/bottle. Again, there are so many regions making superb Cabernet Sauvignons, you may need to taste through some samples to see what you prefer. An earthy Cabernet Franc from Chile, Argentina, or Brazil at or around $25-30/bottle adds another Cabernet to the list without being too repetitive. A silky smooth, yet powerful Petit Verdot from Chile at around $15-25/bottle adds a uniqueness to your list. These wines are crowd pleasers and show stoppers and should not be slept on.

Finishing up with some easy-drinking wines, we have a Pinot Noir from Chile's Casablanca Valley or Argentina's Patagonia at $25-35/bottle. The wine comes from the same notable regions mentioned as when we were selecting a wine by the glass, but this is at a higher price point for those guests hoping to enjoy a bottle with their meals. A Bonarda from Argentina at around $20-30/bottle adds a splash of character to your list. Bonarda is grown particularly in the Mendoza and San Juan regions of Argentina, and it is medium bodied with plushy tannin. Finishing up with a Sangiovese from Argentina, coming in around $15-20/bottle, your wine list has a perfect trio of lighter styles of red wines by the bottle. Finishing on a sweet note, a Late Harvest selection from Argentina from $20-45/bottle* is the final touch to this list. Plenty of these wines are produced, of many different varieties, so it should be easy enough to find.

Chapter 13
AUSTRALIAN INSPIRED WINE LIST TEMPLATE

30 Selections Wine List (Australian Inspired)

SPARKLING Wines—5 Selection
1. Inexpensive Sparkling for cocktails $3-6/bottle*
2. Australian Sparkling $7-12/bottle*
3. Sparkling Rosé $10-16/bottle*
4. Champagne for casual nights $40-50/bottle
5. Celebratory Champagne $50-75/bottle

WHITE WINES–9 Selections
1. Semillon from New South Wales in Australia $7-14/bottle*
2. Sauvignon Blanc from New Zealand $7-14/bottle*
3. Chardonnay from Victoria or Western Australia $8-12/bottle*
4. Pinot Gris from Adelaide Hills or

Tasmania, Australia $8-12/bottle*
5. Riesling from Clare Valley or Eden Valley, Australia $8-12/bottle*
6. Viognier from Barossa Valley or Rutherglen, Australia $20-25/bottle
7. Chardonnay from Victoria or Western Australia $20-30/bottle
8. Chenin Blanc from Swan Valley or Margaret River, Australia $20-30/bottle
9. Marsanne from Barossa Valley, Australia $10-20/bottle

ROSÉ WINES–3 Selections
1. Australian Rosé $10-14/bottle*
2. Provence Rosé $10-12/bottle*
3. Higher End Rosé from Australia $15-25/bottle

RED WINES–12 Selections
1. Malbec from Barossa Valley or Langhorne Creek, Australia $10-14/bottle*
2. Shiraz from Barossa Valley or McLaren Vale, Australia $10-16/bottle*
3. Pinot Noir from Yarra Valley Australia $8-14/bottle*
4. Cabernet Sauvignon from Coonawarra or Margaret River, Australia $8-14/bottle*
5. Grenache from McLaren Vale, Australia $8-12/bottle*
6. Merlot from Australia $12-20/bottle
7. Cabernet Sauvignon from Coonawarra or Margaret River, Australia $20-30/bottle
8. Cabernet Blend from Coonawarra or

How to Build a Wine List

Margaret River, Australia $25-30/bottle
9. Petit Verdot from Margaret River, Australia $15-25/bottle
10. Pinot Noir from New Zealand $25-35/bottle
11. Shiraz from Barossa Valley or McLaren Vale, Australia $20-30/bottle
12. Sangiovese from Victoria, Australia $15-20/bottle

DESSERT WINE–1 Selection
1. Muscat from Australia $20-45/bottle*

For our Australian-inspired menu, we are sticking with five sparkling wines. Our classic inexpensive sparkling for cocktails at $3-6/bottle* is a must for keeping our costs down. An Australian Sparkling from around $7-12/bottle* might come from Tasmania or Yarra Valley or even Adelaide Hills. All of these regions make lovely bubbles. A sparkling rosé for $10-16/bottle* will bring a nice color to the list and can be found in the same regions from Australia, or you can stick with a standard Prosecco. I always have a Champagne for casual nights from $40-50/bottle available for those who are fans of the easily recognized Champagne brands. A Celebratory Champagne most likely from a $50-75/bottle comes from a smaller Grower Champagne house to round out your selection.

Starting with our nine wines, we have a Semillon from New South Wales in Australia for $7-14/bottle*. This grape is growing in popularity in Australia, and is becoming easier to find throughout the world. Other regions produce great ones, but look for those coming from New South Wales first. These are lighter and better recognized. A classic Sauvignon Blanc from New Zealand from $7-14/bottle* is my next pick. There are plenty of nice Sauvignon Blancs being made in Australia, if you prefer to keep it from this region. A chardonnay from Victoria or Western Australia for $8-12/bottle* will add a creaminess and texture to the white wines by-the- glass lineup. A Pinot Gris from Adelaide Hills or Tasmania from Australia at $8-12/bottle* is going to be one of your big sellers. Finish up your glass pours with a Riesling from Clare Valley or Eden Valley in Australia for $8-12/bottle.* These can be found sweet, but mostly are dry.

For white wines offered only by the bottle, Viognier from Barossa Valley or Rutherglen from Australia at $20-25/bottle is a great selection. This grape is not saturating the market yet, but there is enough of it to add to a bottle list. A chardonnay from Victoria or Western Australia with a higher price tag of $20-30/bottle is a great upsell from your chardonnay by the glass. There are chardonnays being made well in other regions, but these are the first two you might have access to. A Chenin Blanc from Swan Valley or Margaret River in Australia at $20-30/bottle is a great addition to the selections already offered. The final touch for white wines is a Marsanne from Barossa Valley at $10-20/bottle. This wine might be a blend, with Marsanne in it, so do not be discouraged if you can only find it mixed with other grapes.

Three rosé wines are my next choices. An Australian Rosé from $10-14/bottle* could include a plethora of grapes from a variety of regions. Taste through what is available to you and select your favorite. A classic Provence Rosé from France at around $10-12/bottle* would be my other glass pour. If you are in slower, colder seasons, you may want to stop pouring one of these until the demand is higher in the warmer months. A higher-end rosé from Australia by-the-bottle option, coming in around $15-25/bottle, is for your guests who want to elevate their experience from the glass pours.

For red wines, there are twelve basic selections. To start

How to Build a Wine List

the glass list, we have a Malbec from Barossa Valley or Langhorne Creek in Australia at $10-14/bottle.* Although not from Argentina, this wine is made beautifully in Australia and should not be skipped over. A Shiraz from Barossa Valley or McLaren Vale in Australia, ranging from $10-16/bottle,* is the next selection. Internationally known, this wine deserves at least one glass pour. A lean Pinot Noir from Yarra Valley in Australia for $8-14/bottle* would add a nice light-bodied option for your guests. You could always find a great option from New Zealand, as well. A bold and powerful Cabernet Sauvignon from Coonawarra or Margaret River in Australia at $8-14/bottle* is up next. Our Cabernet lovers will be keeping an eye out for this one. Finishing up the glass pours, is a Grenache from McLaren Vale in Australia for $8-12/bottle.* This light-bodied wine is deliciously aromatic and will be a sure show stopper.

Moving onto our bottle only list, we have a Merlot from Australia around $12-20/bottle. There are several areas in Australia that grow notable Merlot, including Coonawarra, Yarra Valley, Margaret River, Hunter Valley, and Barossa Valley. I'd recommend a higher-end bottle of Cabernet Sauvignon from Coonawarra or Margaret River from Australia, coming in at $20-30/bottle. I have also chosen a Cabernet Blend from Coonawarra or Margaret River in Australia at $25-30/bottle. There are a lot of blends coming out of all regions in Australia, so pick one that you like the best and have good availability for. A thick and luscious Petit Verdot from Margaret River in Australia at around $15-25/bottle is the next suggestion. This grape is typically blended into wines, but on its own is inky and impressive.

A Pinot Noir from New Zealand, coming in around $25-35/bottle, is my next selection. You could use another Pinot Noir from Australia, but for some variety I chose the wine from New Zealand. A higher-end Shiraz from Barossa Valley or McLaren Vale at $20-30/bottle is an excellent addition to the list. Finishing up our reds with an interesting pick, we have Sangiovese from Victoria in Australia at $15-20/bottle. Sangiovese is a grape most commonly grown in Italy, but these expressions coming out of Victoria are exceptional. Our dessert wine selection is a famous Muscat from Australia at $20-45/bottle.* These sticky-sweet wines are excellent with cookies and ice cream.

Chapter 14
SCALING UP YOUR MENU

If you are hoping for more than just the thirty selections, don't worry. This is the easiest thing to do—once you have an already-established list. You can grow the list before opening. If you are going to gradually add to your menu, wait until you are able to hear from your guests. Get their opinions, and ask what they wish you were serving. You can also pull data and see what is selling better. Maybe it would shock you to find out white wines are selling better than red, or there is more rosé sold than sparkling wine. Be sure to take advantage of this data and implement it in a way that works for you. Make your guests happy, and they will come back more frequently.

If you do not want to wait until you are open and have this data to work from, don't worry. There are many ways to figure out what else should be added to the list. You can taste wines with your distributors and see what you think is delicious and pairs well with your food. You can analyze your menu more. Some of these templates are heavier with red wines than white wines, while others are heavier in whites than reds. The reasoning behind that is cuisine based. If you are serving lighter fare, lighter wines tend to pair better with it. If you are serving heavier foods and you are a BBQ spot, then you might need more heavy wines to go with your food.

Try to find some native grape varietals if you are adding to your Italian list. Some I would look into are Nerello Mascalese, Arneis, Brachetto (sweet), Cannonau, Corvina (or a blend from Valpolicella or Amarone), Dolcetto, Friulano, Grillo, Passerina, Pecorino, Primitivo, or Ribolla Gialla. To mention some additions for a French-inspired wine menu, look into the following regions: Alsace, Jura, Savoie, Beaujolais, etc. For a look into the Southwest French grapes, ask your distributors for a taste of Tannat, Colombard, Petit Manseng, Pinot Blanc, etc. For a classic wine list, you can explore some lesser-represented regions. These areas might not have much demand, but they are often of high quality and low price points. Regions I would not sleep on would be South Africa, Hungary, Austria, and Israel. A dry Furmint from Hungary seems to make its way onto most of my lists with more than thirty selections, and guests love it.

I also make a case for adding local wines onto any menu. No matter where you are, wine is being made, including in all fifty states in the US, and almost all countries at this point. Winemakers tend to hop around the world frequently, so do not assume there are only inexperienced locals making your fermented grape juice. Take time to explore the local wine scene, and select one or two wines to feature on your list. At one point in time, even California was dismissed as a less-than-serious wine-producing region. You never know if your region is the next one to have a moment of fame, and it is best to get in on the ground floor when the prices are affordable. I am currently residing in Pennsylvania, and there is more than one winery creating wines I would seek out on a wine list.

Scale up in a way that is sustainable for your business. Do not spend thousands of dollars on new inventories of wines if you are unable to pay your staff that month. Stay familiar with your numbers. There are a lot of classes available for costing and suggested numbers for your business. So much of today's information is available for free or for an affordable price online. Stay informed and passionate about what you are serving, and others will join you.

Chapter 15
COSTS AND PRICING

Once you have your wines selected, you will need to work on pricing. There are many pricing guides you can find online, and there is not one correct way to do this. The way I like to do it is to keep your wines by the glass at around 20-24% cost of goods sold and your entire bottle list closer to 28%. You will sell primarily wines by the glass, so you can afford a lower price point for sales on bottles. I recommend pouring 5 ounce glasses of wine, as there are just over 25 oz in a 750mL standard bottle of wine, meaning there are 5 glasses per bottle. Here is an example of how to figure out what to charge.

How to Build a Wine List

Style	Wines BTG (5 oz pours)	Cost	Tax & Freight	Total Cost	PRICE to Charge	COGS
Spark	Cava Brut Chic	$ 7.25	$ 0.51	$ 7.76	$ 9.00	17.00%
Spark	Pet-Nat Rosé	$ 13.60	$ 0.95	$ 14.55	$ 13.00	22.08%
Spark	Prosecco	$ 9.52	$ 0.67	$ 10.19	$ 11.00	18.27%
White	Sauvignon Blanc	$ 11.00	$ 0.77	$ 11.77	$ 11.00	21.10%
White	Riesling	$ 10.50	$ 0.74	$ 11.24	$ 9.00	24.62%
White	Pinot Grigio	$ 10.00	$ 0.70	$ 10.70	$ 10.00	21.10%
White	California Chardonnay	$ 9.99	$ 0.70	$ 10.69	$ 11.00	19.17%
Rosé	Provence Rosé	$ 10.00	$ 0.70	$ 10.70	$ 12.00	17.59%
Red	Malbec	$ 9.00	$ 0.63	$ 9.63	$ 9.00	21.10%
Red	Tempranillo	$ 11.50	$ 0.81	$ 12.31	$ 11.00	22.06%
Red	Pinot Noir	$ 13.50	$ 0.95	$ 14.45	$ 12.00	23.74%
Red	Cabernet Sauvignon	$ 12.50	$ 0.88	$ 13.38	$ 12.00	21.98%
Red	Zinfandel	$ 10.50	$ 0.74	$ 11.24	$ 11.00	20.15%
				Average COGS BTG		20.86%

This is an imaginary wine list, but this chart was easy enough to create in Sheets or Excel. You put the cost in the column following the wine, then account for freight and tax. These numbers vary drastically, depending on which state or country you are in. Once you have the total cost of your wine, you can divide it by 25.35 to get how much an ounce will cost you. When you have that number, you can multiply it by the amount you decided to pour for your glasses. In this case, that would be 5. Take that number and multiply it by 100. The next number you will use is what you decide you want your COGS to be. In this case, we take 20. The number left will be what you need to charge to get to 20 percent COGS. You can round this number up or down, depending on your business strategy.

$10 bottle / 25.35 = 0.39 x 5 = 1.9724 x 100 = 197.24 / 20 = $9.86
Round up to $10/glass = 21.10% COGS.

Figuring out bottle prices is a lot easier than glasses. You do not need to worry about how much each ounce costs, but you'll focus on the total bottle price and what you would sell it for. An easy rule of thumb is to multiply the bottle by 3, and you will come out with around 30 percent cost. Wine lists, however, are not this cut and dry. Your menu should be organic and always changing. If a higher-end bottle of wine is $300 for you to buy, you will not want to charge $900 to your guests. While the percentage might be around 30 percent cost, the $600 upcharge is not really warranted. You can *maybe* double the price, but even that might be a stretch. I would suggest just charging $100 more. While selling this bottle for $400 might have your costs coming in at a whopping 75%, that $100 of revenue is the equivalent of selling 4 bottles of wine at $33/bottle with a cost percentage of 30 percent. At the end of the day, dollars in revenue is what will pay your bills, not your percentage.

All these numbers are completely up to you to control. I had a client once who told me he wanted his COGS to be 28-35 percent, so he could be more attainable as a casual, everyday-dining experience. You know your market better than anyone after some research. See what your competition is selling their wine for. Don't price yourself out of the market in an effort to chase down the most money. Don't price too low and have people wonder why you are so cheap. There are many systems that can do the actual costing for you, so there is little need to reach for a calculator these days. Know that your business model depends on your wine-and-beverage program to optimize costs to turn a larger profit. Treat your wine list seriously, not as an afterthought, and it can make you a good deal of money.

Chapter 16
CAN YOU USE ARTIFICIAL INTELLIGENCE FOR YOUR WINE LIST?

There are a lot of different "AI bots" coming into the market, and you might want to see how to utilize them for your menu. One thing that might come in handy is asking which popular grapes are being sold in the region. One of the shortcomings of these systems is that they do not have up-to-date data, but run two to three years behind. You can ask ChatGPT (WWW.openAI.com) for tasting notes for your wines, or you can ask what wines should be on your list.

Asking a bot about tasting notes will give you generalized responses. They will not know that one Cabernet Sauvignon is going to be leaner in style and perhaps a little more green on the nose than another Cabernet Sauvignon, which will be more fruity and heavier. Instead, tasting notes will be an average of all Cabernet Sauvignons. If you are writing tasting notes under your wines on your lists (I like to do this whenever possible), you can use these notes as a starting point, but reference the winemaker's notes for the specific wines you have selected as well.

If you want to use AI to generate your entire wine list, I recommend asking very specific questions to do so. Questions like "can you write me a wine list?" will result in not-great selections. Asking questions like "can you write me a wine list with wines only from South America, featuring ten selections, organized first by style and then by grape varietal" will get you much better results. AI tends to also give responses with specific wines from actual popular wineries. This is also not helpful, as AI does not have access to what is available in your market. You could also ask for a tasting note for a specific wine and include a small description under each selection. AI can write a long note when you ask for a simple tasting note, but can also keep it to three to four words if you specify what you want.

While these technologies are still in the developmental stages, they are very good at math. You can ask what you should charge for a glass of wine that costs you X amount of dollars, and it will spit out a couple numbers for you. Always take what these computers say with a grain of salt, and do your own research. While I was playing with it to see if it could make a comprehensive wine list that was Italian inspired it listed Chianti and Sangiovese. I pointed out to the bot they were the same grape, and it apologized and corrected itself. Mistakes like this you might not catch unless you are familiar with wine.

I recommend using these bots only for math and pricing, as well as suggestions for which grapes or styles of wine are selling well. Nothing replaces market research and actually going around to look at other wine menus, but having two-year-old data at the tips of your fingers does not hurt.

Chapter 17
MORE RESOURCES TO LEARN

There are a ton of additional resources I suggest for learning about wine. If you want to collect more knowledge about wine to help build your list even larger, there are many I recommend.

The Society of Wine Educators website does a phenomenal job of setting expectations for their classes and certifications. Their team teaches classes online that you can take before signing up for a local testing center at your own pace. You can choose which class works best for you, and select the time and date to take the exam. The books you purchase have all the possible testing information provided with the most up to date data. Even if you are hoping to study before the classes start, you can buy the books online whenever you want. They have multiple levels of wine certifications, and they offer certifications for spirits as well. Their offered exams are Certified Specialist of Wine (CSW), Certified Wine Educator (CWE), Certified Specialist of Spirits (CSS), and Certified Spirits Educator (CSE). You can find their information on their easy-to-navigate website. There is an application for iOS and Android called Wine Quiz from the Society of Wine Educators, which I highly recommend downloading. It is free, and the quizzes are excellent.

The Wine and Spirits Education Trust (WSET) is an internationally recognized association. Their program is one that works toward the Master of Wine certification. I recommend these classes for beginners, as the classroom settings make for a great learning environment. When I travel abroad, a vast majority of people only recognize this certification. If you are hoping to move around in your career and work in a multitude of countries, this is the course I would tell you to take. Their exams are offered in wine, sake, and spirits. For wine classes, they offer Level 1, Level 2, Level 3, and Level 4 (Diploma). Once you complete your diploma, you can apply for their Master of Wine program.

WineFolly is a helpful website for beginning wine lovers, as well. They have their own maps and graphs, which are some of the best to look at and learn from in the industry. If you are a visual learner, chances are you will want to look through their website and courses. Their social-media pages are also great learning tools. Madeline Puckette is the founder and has made a career of making wine approachable for the masses. She and Christine Marsiglio (Master of Wine) offer their own certifications, and although I have not taken them myself, I have only heard great feedback.

There are a few podcasts I enjoy listening to, including "Wine for Normal People." Please note, I think the content in this podcast is actually super in depth, and industry professionals can learn a lot from listening. Elizabeth Schneider is the author of the book *Wine for Normal People*, and I will admit, she is one of the best storytellers I have found in the industry. She also offers classes on her website. As I have never taken them (why not take one?), I cannot speak to it, but if her podcast is any indication, you will be in great hands. Another fun podcast is "You're Gonna Need a Bigger Bottle," hosted by Scott Hudson and Jamie Harrison Rubin, where they pair movies with wines.

My own book, *Pairing Paws: Dog Breeds and Their Spirit Wines* is a cute read. This book pairs wines with dog breeds, based on their similar characteristics. Although it does make a beautiful coffee-table book, with full pages of dogs photographed, it also contains great information about some of the wineries and winemaking. Whatever your source, there are multiple avenues you can take to reach your goal of learning more about wine. Taking business classes can also help with the business part of your goal. Keep learning, and you will become better and better at managing your beverage program.

Chapter 18
ORDERING

Placing an opening order will be a little trickier because you do not have any data about what sort of volume you are anticipating. A lot depends on your market and how many seats your restaurant has. I recommend only a few bottles of your more expensive wines, as they tend not to sell as frequently as the less expensive ones. About your wines by the glass, have at least one case per fifty restaurant seats to prevent running out of anything. Wines by the glass you will eventually sell, so it is not a bad thing to over-order. Your systems will help you track how much you sell, and you can adjust your ordering and par sheets based on this data.

Keep an eye on your wines, and make sure none of them go bad before you are able to sell them. Rosé wines tend not to last much longer than a year or two after buying them, so don't stock up on these wines during colder months. As a general rule of thumb, lighter wines tend to sell better in warmer months, and heavier wines sell better in colder months. Try to plan your ordering accordingly. Your red wines are typically able to outlast your white wines in the cellar, so keep that in mind if you intend to over-order to have extra product in stock.

How to Build a Wine List

Hopefully, your cellar or storage area is a dark-and-cooler location. Ideally a wine fridge, but you could also have a fine closet or walk-in for them. 55 degrees and 75 percent humidity are the magic numbers to strive for, but in general, keep the wine away from excessive heat and light. Keep your bottles stored on their sides, and a few months at room temperature will not destroy them.

Some restaurant systems are now monitoring how many glasses and bottles are sold and spitting out an easy-to-use order for your managers to place. Be sure to place your orders in a time frame that works for your distributors best. As a rule of thumb, I try to pick one day to count what I have in house and place the order. It is best to pull figures from your point of sale system as well as double check with your managers what is in house. Check if there are any holidays in the upcoming week that might positively or negatively impact your business. Ask your bartenders if there was any breakage you need to account for. Try to keep your hands as active in the beverage program as possible.

Chapter 19
PAIRINGS

There are many ways to pair wines with your food. I would recommend working with your chef for this part of designing a wine list.

If you want to add a "suggested pairing" to your menu, there are many ways to go about it. You will need to try the wines with the food before recommending it together, as some pairings work better in theory than in practice.

The easiest way to pair wines with food is to match the body and have complementary flavors. The body of the wine is determined by the "mouthfeel" or texture of the wine in your mouth. Think about the difference between skim milk, two percent milk, and whole milk. The skim milk would be equivalent to your light bodied wine, the two percent would be medium bodied, and the whole milk would be full bodied. You would pair the lighter wines with lighter dishes, medium bodied wines with moderate weighted foods, and heavier wines with more substantial foods.

Complementary flavors are another way to pair your wine and food. If you have a New Zealand Sauvignon Blanc with major citrus notes, it will pair nicely with a ceviche with citrus juices. If your wine has tomato notes, it will pair well with fresh tomatoes or a dish with tomato sauce. This method could be used in the cooking process as well. If you are braising a leg of lamb in Cabernet Sauvignon, you can pair it easily with a Cabernet Sauvignon, as the notes in the dish will echo those in the food.

Contrasting pairings is another idea for wine pairings. If you have a dish that is particularly spicy, it might need a wine with some sweetness to balance and tone down the spice. If one dish is oozing with fat, it might behoove you to match it with a high-acid, bright wine to cut through the fattiness. Fried and salty foods tend to be a great example of this, pairing exceptionally with Champagne, Rieslings, and other high-acid wines. One of my favorite Champagne pairings is any snack that ends in -itos, with those cheese powders and salt setting off the brightness and bubbles in the wine beautifully. There was a trend a few years ago pairing sweet chocolates with dry red wines, which is another example of contrasting pairings.

The reason I recommend trying the wine with the food before printing a pairing menu is because there is normally more than one item on your plate you need to think about. Yes, that Merlot might pair beautifully with a beef tenderloin, but it would be disastrous with the artichoke hearts fried on the side. That tuna carpaccio with soy-miso glaze sounded perfect with the lean Pinot Bianco until the sauce beat up your delicate aromatics in the wine. There is no substitution for tasting the pairings before printing.

Chapter 20
EXTRA WINE LIST TIPS

As a wine professional, nothing is more discouraging than a wine list that is out of date. If your guests order a bottle of wine and it is out of stock, it might set the mood of their entire meal. Some guests have demanded I give them a more expensive bottle for free after such a mistake (I did not do that). Keep your menu as up to date as possible. If you are out of a wine, remove it from the list until it comes back into stock. If you are printing your menus, this might be costly. A lot of restaurants have virtual wine lists these days to save printing costs. These electronic lists can always be up to date without costing you anything.

Have a designer make your list look extra nice. If you cannot afford to hire one, there are tons of online templates you can purchase on Etsy or Koji that use Canva. Your wine list can be easily changed in software like Canva or InDesign. Having a menu that looks pleasing is half the battle of sales. If you have space to add a description of what each wine tastes like, I've found this vastly helps sell the wines.

Budget for your wines. If you are trying to add new wines to the menu, set yourself a budget and calculate it out before placing the order. It is easy to spend more than you anticipated on wines when you are not keeping track of them.

Do not have a collection of wines at the same price point in the same category unless there is an easy distinction. For example, there is no reason for a wine list to have six selections of a $45 bottle Pinot Grigio. This will do nothing but clutter your wine list and confuse your guests.

Inventory of your wines should be taken monthly at least. If your beverage manager is bonused on costs, make sure someone else is doing the counting. Spot check whoever counts inventory to make sure it is as accurate as possible. Some restaurants I worked in had a system where they only ordered what they had an empty bottle for. This one-for-one exchange tried to eliminate staff from stocking up on products they did not need and/or over-ordering.

The biggest determining factor for the by the glass versus a bottle selection is pricing. If your market could tolerate a wine priced at $40/glass, then you have a larger swing of what you can pour by the glass. If your market is off put by a wine that is more than $10/glass, you will need to sell your more expensive wines by the bottle.

Distributors are happy to help you build your wine list, as they're mostly paid with a commission of their sales. Pending laws in your state, they might be able to support your list with tastings, or sponsored events. Sometimes distributors could bring free products to showcase at an event you are throwing. Just make sure you are not asking for free goods without a mutually beneficial situation. Distributors should have "sell sheets" or "tech sheets" on all of their products, which you can ask for to distribute to your staff.

Reviews and changes to the wine list I like to tackle at least twice a year. Changing with the seasons might be a little too frequent and will cause disruptions as your staff struggles to adjust to the new seasonal food and cocktails. I prefer to bulk together the cold seasons (fall and winter) and the warm seasons (spring and summer). You can use these changes to rotate wines that are not selling as well and try your hand at something new.

Know that you are in control of your business, and you have the ability to succeed without hiring a beverage manager; it just will take some work on your part. You can put together a wonderfully cohesive wine list without spending thousands of dollars on a consultant. Remember to follow the steps outlined in this book, and you are sure to have a wine list that makes sense for your guests as well as hit your financial goals. If you have more questions or would like to connect with me, reach out. I am confident with this book you can put together a wine menu that will optimize your profits and make your guests happy.

Acknowledgments

There are many people without whom, this book would not have been possible.

First and foremost: I would not be where I am today without the love and support of my family. Thank you for the unwavering support. Thank you, dad, for reading and helping with the business side.

To Zakary Edington, the man who is my constant companion. Words cannot express how thankful I am for you.

To the Sommelier Community: I have always been honored to be amongst you, thank you for welcoming me into such a loving and caring support system.

To all of my friends for being the most supporting and loving people, thank you.

To all of those who have had an impact on my career, there are too many of you to name, but you know who you are, from the bottom of my heart, thank you.

About the Author

Michele Gargiulo is a Certified Sommelier from the Court of Master Sommeliers, a WSET Diploma student (currently Advanced), a Certified Sake Advisor from the Sake School of America, an Executive Bourbon Steward from the Stave and Thief Society, and a Certified Specialist of Wine from the Society of Wine Educators.

She graduated from The Culinary Institute of America, and prior to that studied Genetics at Rutgers University. She was the Teaching Assistant for the Wines Class at The Culinary Institute of America for a year under Professor Weiss, and has taught wine classes at Montgomery Culinary Institute. She was the beverage director for multiple successful restaurants. Michele was named amongst Philly Mag's New Faces of Wine in 2017 and was written about in many other magazines, as well as press appearances on news stations.

She has made her career about making wine more approachable and fun for those who are too intimidated to learn more. She often pairs wine with things that others would not think to, like art, music, feelings, and now, dogs!

To learn more visit:
http://www.michelegargiulo.com

Also by Michele Gargiulo

Pairing Paws: Dog Breeds and Their Spirit Wines

Pairing Paws: Cat Breeds and Their Spirit Wines (Coming Summer 2023)

www.ingramcontent.com/pod-product-compliance
Lightning Source LLC
LaVergne TN
LVHW010428070526
838199LV00066B/5955